I. NOUNS

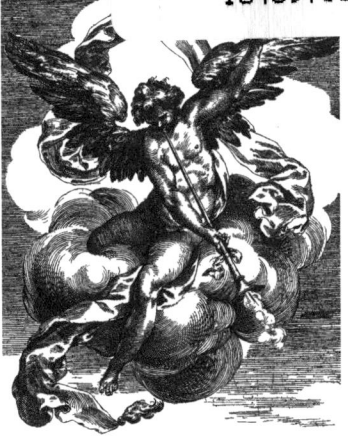

- SHAMAN FIRE
- KISS ME IT'S APRIL
- MY NEIGHBOR IS A GOBLIN
- HELICOPTER MOM
- SHE'S MY "ROOMMATE"
- CONVERSATIONS WITH STUDENTS
- ODE TO CARMENCITA
- ORANGES & BABY GATORS
- EARLY MORNING IN TAMPA FL
- BUS STOP THOUGHTS
- THE ART OF FALLING IN LOVE WITH BOYS
- FIN

II. TWIN FLAMES & A TSUNAMI

- DISCOVERY AS AN ACT OF REBELLION
- I HAVE BECOME A PLAGUE UPON YOU
- WITNESSED
- UNWOUND
- NON-PRACTICING POLYAMORIST
- ARIES
- EL ARREPENTIMIENTO
- LOVE WITCH IN ACTION
- LOVE ON LOAN
- TWIN FLAME RUNNER
- MORE THAN SORRY
- OBSERVACIÓN DE LA CÓLERA
- THE HIEROPHANT & THE THREE OF SWORDS
- TOWNSFOLK
- LOST IN TRANSLATION

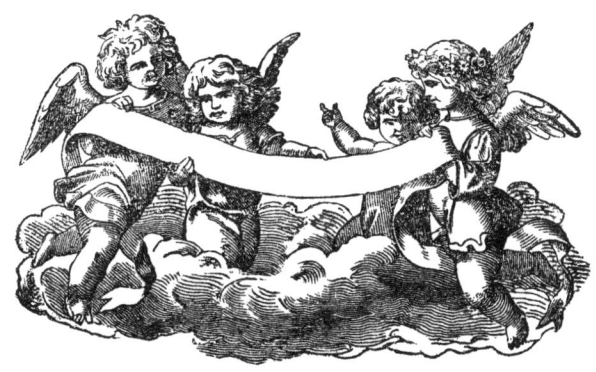

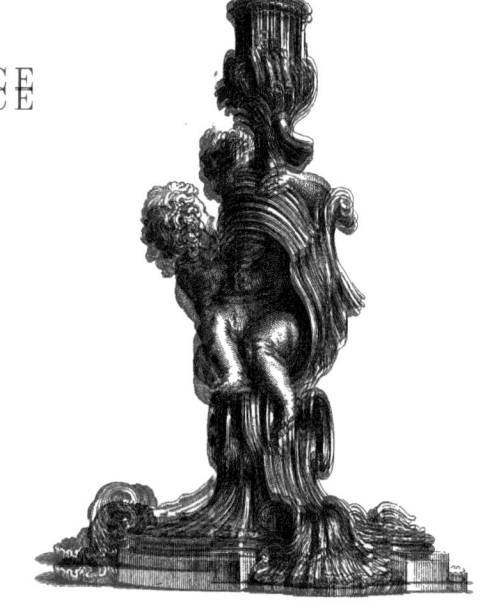

I.
NOUNS: PEOPLE, PLACES, THINGS

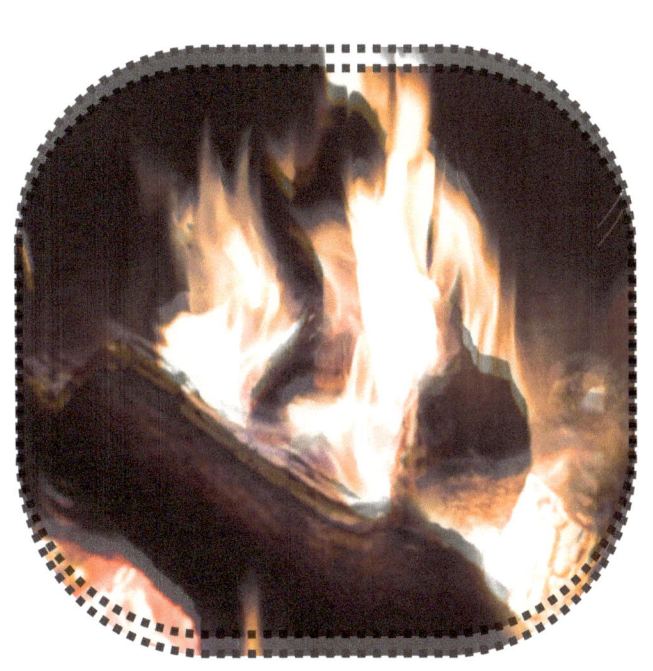

In Spring plant seeds and learn
In Summer apply knowledge and tend the growth
In Autumn harvest food and the fruits of applications
In Winter Rejoice and Reflect
With the New Year start again

:SHAMAN FIRE:

08/2021

The land of sand is behind me
Carved limestone walls
Rush past my window

I
Passenger &
Newcomer &
Stranger to the corn

The Shamans,
The voracious & wild ones,
The curse breakers.
They who wield
The tools they
Smelt in the forge
Of their own infernal
Shadow Work,

Remind me,
That I am no visitor,
That all of me is welcome,
That we have all been here before.

That I am enough as I am.

Remind me,
That the Fire cares not,
Needs not,
To know.
That Fire cares only to do
As Fire does

Warm
Rage
Consume
Live
Nourish
Transform
Revive
Restore &
Burn
On& on& on…

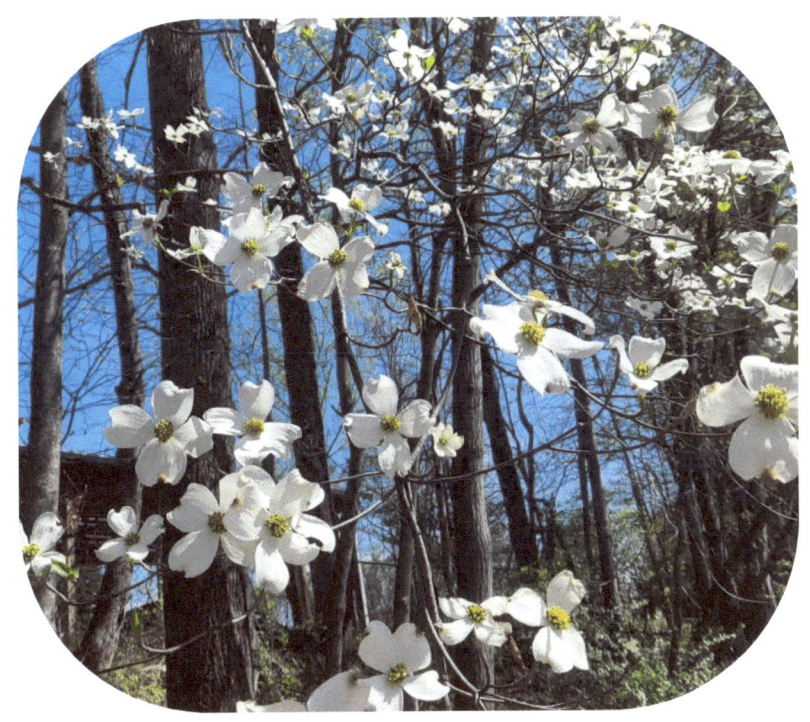

KISS ME IT'S APRIL

04/16/2024

April always brings out
The aggressive romantic in me.
The flowers cast their magic
The winds play with the trees.
My dreams become vivid technicolor,
I dream of you and me.
My hands pray for hard work to find them.
The grass is reaching out for rain.
I sit with Patience in these woods
I say, "Now I am ready to wait."
We watch the sprouts together
The buds and blossoms grow
The sprouts push through the soil
They are not imprisoned anymore
I say, "I've been waiting for you, my love."
Then I look up at the sky.
Patience pats me on the back, says,
"You asked me once, 'Why wait?'
Well, this is why."

MY NEIGHBOR IS A GOBLIN:

MY NEIGHBOR IS A GOBLIN:

12/2024

12/2024

They have pockets full
Of treats and stones
Their eyes are soft & blue as pools
And every time they rummage
They find something good for you

That goblin is a spit fire
A boiling pot
In a warm kitchen
On a cold day
A wide open door
Little cakes on display

I asked them for sugar yesterday
They gave me a pie
It has sacred angel numbers
& Geometry baked inside

They have blackbirds on their tree
The very best, very warm hugs
I thought I'd write them a poem
So I could show them my love

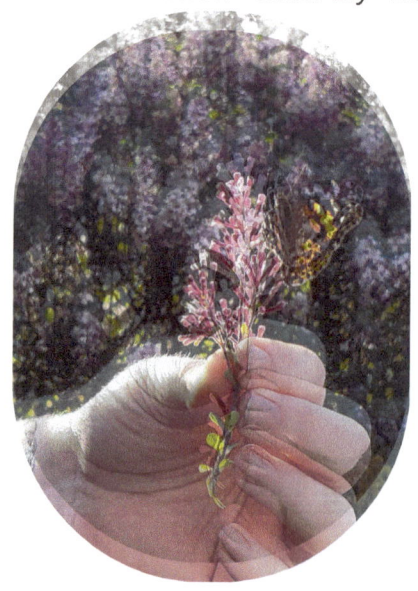

HELICOPTER MOM

6/21/2023

Daughter dances to the beat
Of Mother's drum
Daughter splashes paint all over her canvas

Daughter lounges in the sun
Watches the clouds
Tells stories to the dandelions
Crocuses and toads

Daughter watches the water
Mother once rescued herself from
Daughter sees nothing but ripples from
Fishes Kisses
This is Mother's hard work

SHE'S MY "ROOMMATE"

08/14/2013

"What do you mean?"
Her forefingers were tracing the rim of her tumbler,
the only sound in the room now was the crackle of her ice cubes.
We are melting away in a pool of single-malt whiskey.
-, eyes ever on her feet, replied to her with silence.
"I'll have what she's having," she said.
I grinned at her, "You don't even know what I'm drinking, baby."
When I say I don't have time
It means
I'd rather right a poem after
I
Write a poem
When I say
I don't want to talk about it
I actually mean to
Inform you
That
I know you don't want to hear
What I have to say
So
Why should I waste my time
With the babblers
When I'm sleepy?
Go away,
Be mortified,
The cannibals
Have readied the spit,
Be horrified,
Beasts have burst free,
The stars no longer glow,
The clouds are naked pagans harboring the snow.

I am a pilgrim
I am an infant
We all are but wounded crows
Broken by hunger woes.
This was all not meant but spoken,
Heart strings once played, now broken,
Forever frozen over,
Avalanche my cover
My oven bakes nothing now
My flames cast no shadows
My words hollow wind blown sorrows

I know a girl toothless smile
Kept a jar full of teeth
Charged five dollars for her sweets
Handles cock like treats
Spread her legs like butterfly wings
The little children that live
Within the men and women
Are fashioned from the stuff that answers prayers
And fit within themselves
like Russian dolls
Perpetually amazed by brightness
Inspired always by the unending newness of all things
That exist outside themselves
They are enveloped by fascination
Constant pupils of the cosmic academy
Coursing like conscious capillaries
Teeming humanoid parasitic swarms
We have mastered enough to know
That we will always be wrong
That we will die having neglected our time
And our true spirit
Having been ungrateful for living our lives as ourselves
A whole species on a carousel
Murdering and muttering mute incantations
Of change

CONVERSATIONS W/ STUDENTS
CONVERSATIONS W/ STUDENTS

12/2023
12/2023

John is five
John is five
John asked me
John asked me

"What are you doing?"
"What are you doing?"

I told John,
I told John,
"I'm writing a poem."
"I'm writing a poem."

John asked me,
John asked me,
"What is a poem?"
"What is a poem?"

I stopped my pen.
I stopped my pen.
I look at him
I look at him
"A piece of me that
"A piece of me that
Must be shared."
Must be shared."

He wrinkled his brow.
He wrinkled his brow.
"What are you sharing?"
"What are you sharing?"

I say,
I say,
"The music that echoes within me,
"The music that echoes within me,
The shouting of my mind,
The shouting of my mind,
A marionette show of my secrets
A marionette show of my secrets
& The things I cannot hide."
& The things I cannot hide."

"Who are you sharing with?"
"Who are you sharing with?"

I said,
I said,
"Anyone that can read."
"Anyone that can read."

John asked,
John asked,
"Why would you do that?"
"Why would you do that?"

I said,
I said,
"They might feel like me
"They might feel like me
And now they aren't alone,
And now they aren't alone,
Though they might be afraid,
Though they might be afraid,
They could find familiarity or comfort
They could find familiarity or comfort
Right here on this page."
Right here on this page."

ODE TO CARMENCITA

My grandmother was an amazon
Her opinions echoed
Her dance was hers alone
She knew that, she knew it and
It was no secret
Her dance was a poem
Her home was a page that she had written upon
Her family was her story, she was both bard and minstrel
Her love was god of her dreams
Her love kept no secrets
Her love was a closet full of comfy blankets
And she covered us all
My grandmother loved me
The way a tree loves its blossoms
Loves it's branches
The way a tree loves it's fruit
And the seasons that have cradled it
Her love was like that
She loved the way roots
Love the earth that hugs them
She loved
This woman
She loved
She gave me her guitar when I was
Eleven years old
And then
She played
"Yesterday" by The Beatles
She sang the lyrics
Her Cuban accent
Her eyes closed
Her fingers strummed on memories
Her tongue forgot some words

On Sundays
The smell of pig skin, plantains, fried onions
The smell of cigars, cigarettes, burning Myrrha
The smell of her perfume
When my grandmother died
She was so small
A bald being in a hospital bed
Smoking cigarettes that were just
Post-chemotherapy hallucinations
Drinking glasses of whiskey that weren't there
My grandmother in her hospital bed
Was not dying
She was transcending into goddess-hood

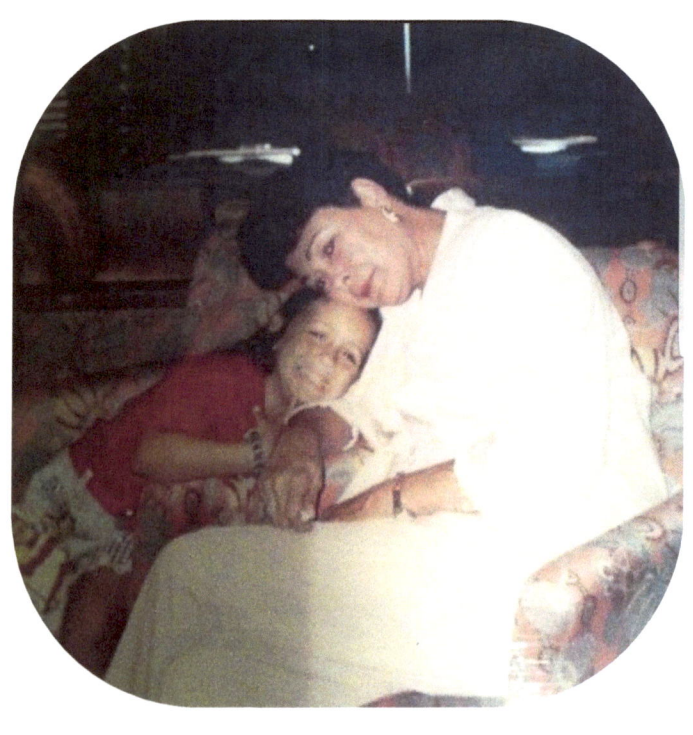

ORANGES & BABY GATORS

08/2014

Today I wrote a poem
It's in the shape of Florida and it smells
Like barbecue
I'm not sure what to call it
I guess "poem" will have to do
I remember planting
poems only when I found
I could not sleep
Writing letters to
My dreams
Insomnia
I don't need you any more
I am living now
I have Life
I'm not expecting
Constrictors to rise from the gorge

EARLY MORNING IN TAMPA FL

11/2015

Blue moon and morning cardinals.
Blue moon and the 45 takes me
Passed pirate coliseums
The braided children are really
Gods in disguise
on the bus
Under a blue moon

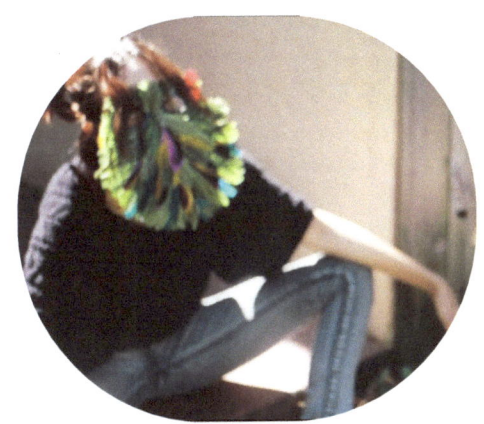

BUS STOP THOUGHTS

06/2014

Fog on north 51 street
Every street lamp is a Jupiter
Unto itself

THE ART OF FALLING IN LOVE WITH L
~~THE ART OF FALLING IN LOVE WITH BOYS~~

2007
2007

Out here everything is mistaken for love
Out here everything is mistaken for love
We wander amidst the sway of lively palm trees
We wander amidst the sway of lively palm trees
& the cool of a starless night
& the cool of a starless night
Still celestial in all its brilliance
Still celestial in all its brilliance
But dulled by the lack of romance in the air
But dulled by the lack of romance in the air
The streets are lined with fallen mangos
The streets are lined with fallen mangos
I pick one up & count the rough, rotten, black spots
I pick one up & count the rough, rotten, black spots
That grace the smooth reds & oranges of the mango hide
That grace the smooth reds & oranges of the mango hide
But when the skin is peeled away
But when the skin is peeled away
Revealing the flawlessly sweet meat that
Revealing the flawlessly sweet meat that
Sticks between my teeth & makes me salivate for more
Sticks between my teeth & makes me salivate for more
I wish for no other fruit to wet my lips with its nectar
I wish for no other fruit to wet my lips with its nectar
I wish for no other meat to slide so delectably over my tongue
I wish for no other meat to slide so delectably over my tongue
Until I glimpse *carambolla, limoncillo, naranja, papaya, mamey*
Until I glimpse *carambolla, limoncillo, naranja, papaya, mamey*
Or the temptation crosses me to break open *la granada*
Or the temptation crosses me to break open *la granada*
& consume its juicy, bitter seeds
& consume its juicy, bitter seeds
I wipe my hands on my worn jeans
I wipe my hands on my worn jeans
& my mouth with the back of my soft sleeve
& my mouth with the back of my soft sleeve
My feet keep in stride
My feet keep in stride
One foot after the other but sometimes
One foot after the other but sometimes
I leap with both feet at the same time
I leap with both feet at the same time
Spinning in all directions, *mareada*
Spinning in all directions, *mareada*
Throwing my head back like a satiated beast
Throwing my head back like a satiated beast
I laugh behind the back of the world
I laugh behind the back of the world
Because I can feel it's tectonic plates sliding beneath my *chancletas*
Because I can feel it's tectonic plates sliding beneath my *chancletas*
As I pluck its flowers to adorn my curls and waves
As I pluck its flowers to adorn my curls and waves
Placing bright purple *orquídeas* behind my ear
Placing bright purple *orquídeas* behind my ear
Or between my breasts
Or between my breasts
To bring out the green in my eyes
To bring out the green in my eyes
For you to fall in love with
For you to fall in love with

Fin: They Hate Women
Fin: They Hate Women

09/2022
09/2022

He cried witch,
He cried witch,
They raised their pitchforks &
They raised their pitchforks &
torches above the
torches above the
Brothers, hoods & banners
Brothers, hoods & banners
Brandished so high
Brandished so high
Though
Though
In the night
In the night
Nothing gleams
Nothing gleams

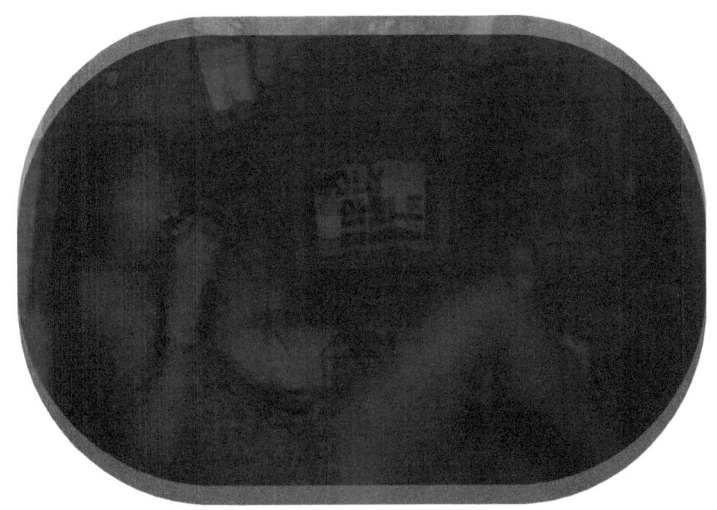

II.
TWIN FLAMES
&
A TSUNAMI

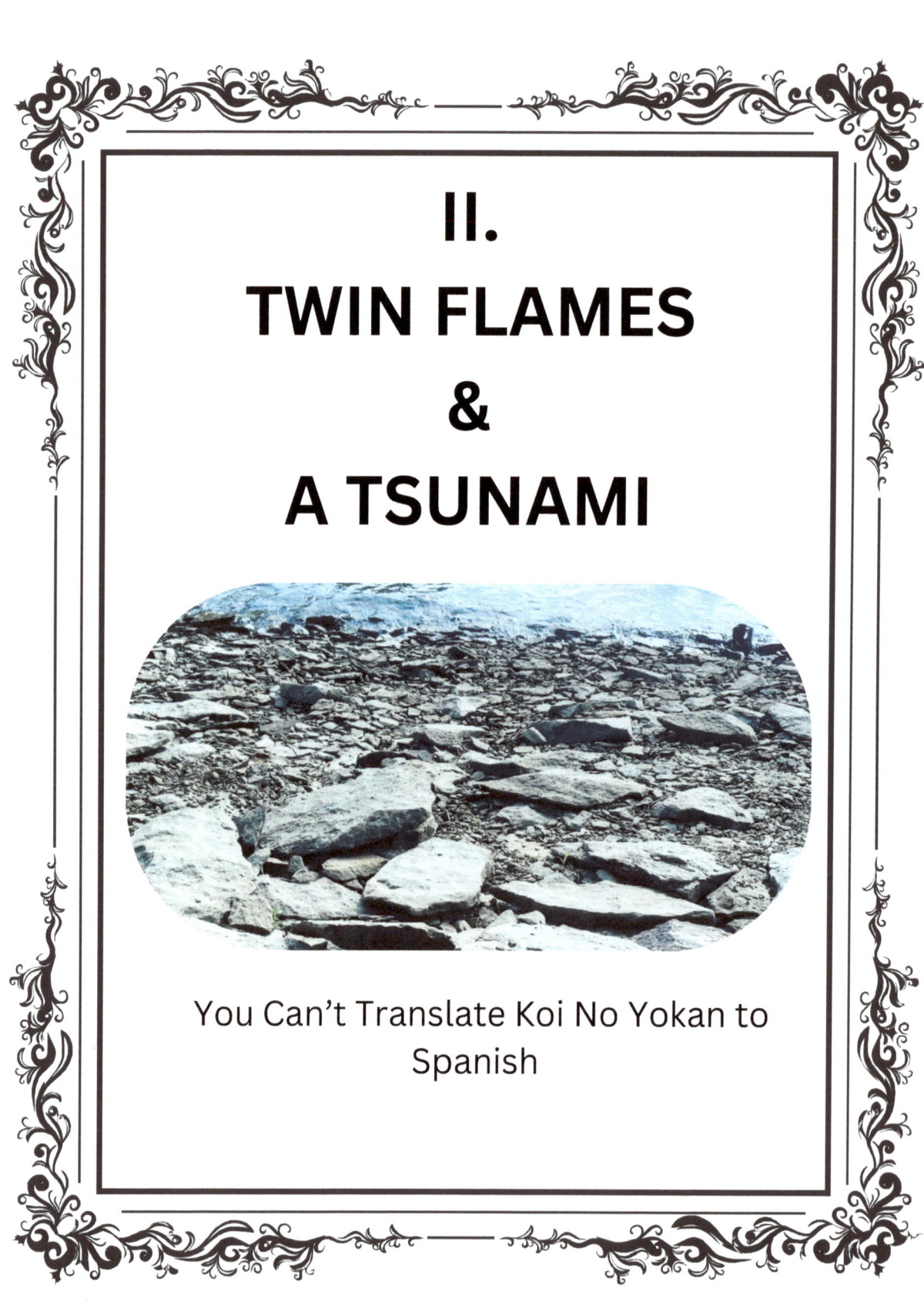

You Can't Translate Koi No Yokan to Spanish

DISCOVERY AS AN ACT OF REBELLION

09/2023

Ah, something has been found
Dropped in the tall grass
Tossed aside
Covered
Cooked
Changed

oh!
A pair of butterflies
Artifacts in the grass
Turquoise sand

And there it lay
A thing needed and lost
When it's found
There is nothing like the remembering

Fall is here
Yet the leaves are still green
The change in the air
Is a change in us

Us,
A pair of butterflies

I'd write you songs
Hand over what I have found
Give you this gift

I'd wait so long inside
This prayer for freedom

I'd slice through fields of tall grass
To find whatever else
We have lost

I HAVE BECOME A PLAGUE UPON YOU OR:
How Curiosity Sheered the Goat

BECOME A PLAGUE UPON YOU OR:
Curiosity Sheered the Goat

07/2023

07/2023

I think you really meant it
When you sent it
But now you want to take it back
It was unironic all along
I know you know
That I know
I know that since
That first chimney log was lit
And the spring night
Wrapped around us
I have been
Dancing in that fire's memory
Circles through your head

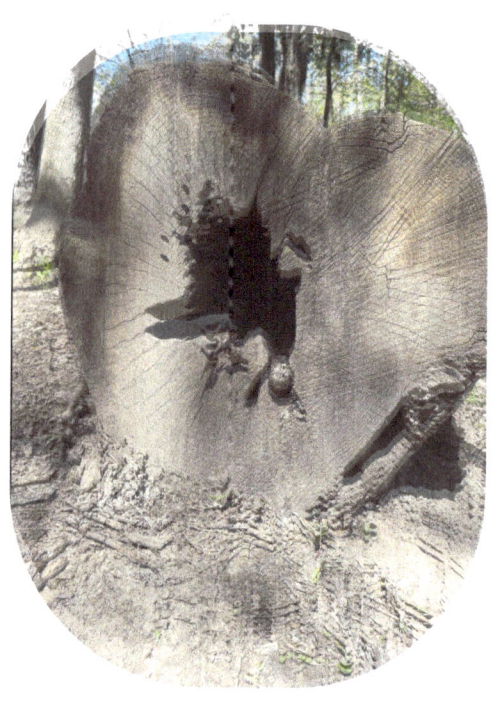

I know you blink away
At the specs of sand
Kicked up by my feet
That bounced to the beat
Of the drum you took up

I know, you took up that drum
So that I would dance for you

I know that you have been thinking of me
More and more and more
I know, I know your secrets

We are the same
You and I
This did not plague me so before those days
I realized our eye color is the same

When you sent me
Such words
By surprise
You became guilty
Of the selfish curiosity it takes
To stick your hand inside my fire
Curious to know
What it would feel like to be burned

WITNESSED
WITNESSED

8/2023
8/2023

Fires, roaring
Fires, roaring
Flames leaping
Flames leaping

I see
I see

Shadow &
Shadow &
Firelight
Firelight
In the wild
In the wild
Electric night
Electric night
Northern drums meet with
Northern drums meet with
Southern hips
Southern hips

You've orchestrated all of this
You've orchestrated all of this
The rushing of my blood
The rushing of my blood
The fluttering of my heart
The fluttering of my heart
The beat
The beat
Within my chest
Within my chest
A thousand *cucuyos*
A thousand *cucuyos*
Springing upwards all
Springing upwards all
Green eyes & glowing
Green eyes & glowing

You peek in and see my face
You peek in and see my face
Flushed cheeks from
Flushed cheeks from
The poetry you sent me
The poetry you sent me
The eyes that glance at me
The eyes that glance at me
The stare, your hands
The stare, your hands

I'm captured
I'm captured

Play that drum
Play that drum
You know
You know
I will dance for you
I will dance for you

You know what you are doing
You know what you are doing
And I wish
And I wish
You'd never stop
You'd never stop

UNWOUND

12/2023

I am still haunted by you

You are in my blood

In my teeth
Under my hair
Behind my eyelids

A shadow softness

A stolen kiss

You are a song
Looping like
Yarn around itself

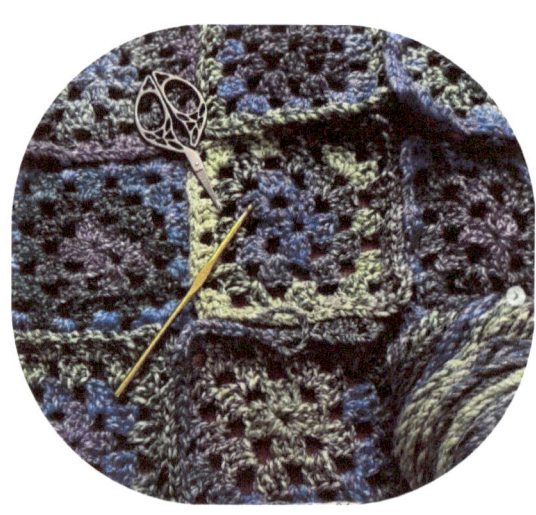

I've knit a sweater
From fibers
Plucked like
Worms
Hidden,
Huddled

I crochet a
Scarf
A bridge
A voodoo doll

I make a coaster
Of my love
Set your cup here
Darling
I want to watch
You sip

NON-PRACTICING POLYAMORIST

1/3/2024

An engorged heart
Immensely so
Unctuous & unnerving

Leisurely & dense
Dusty smoke
Slithering up &
Up &
Stuffy scent of
Patchouli
Stains the ceiling
Venus twinkles
A lit candle
Distant drumming
Dusk is tucked in twilight
Love me and let me Love

I wrap each one
Copper, Silver & Gold
Each love is a stone
Three kings that sing unto my soul

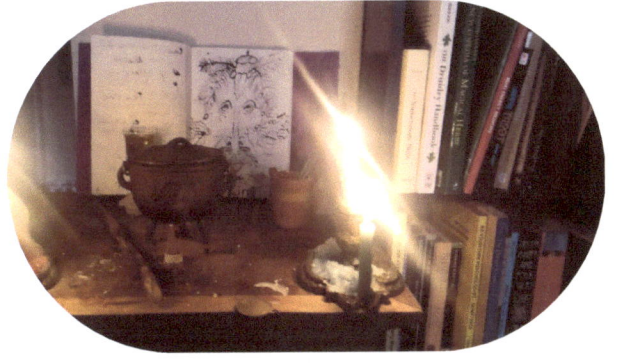

With him I have
Soldiered, birthed & braved
The second a
Twin zap of thunder & flames
The distant third
Weaves a web of virtual yearning
From state to state
& back again to our quiet rooms

I write letters to each one
I swallow syllables down
My belly becomes a
Pool of ink and pulp

To Venus, twinkling
I light
Many candles
That is all
That I can do

ARIES

2007 (edit 01/2024)

More than smoke

Smoldering shadow
Sheepskin & Ram horn
Incense plumes on
Spun wool
Clambering
Climbing
Bleating & Baaing
Yelling at the ceiling
Ignorantly thinking
That flat plain of concrete over my head
Could ever be the sky
Today
I take nothing less
Than anything
I desire
I will become the fire
If it pleases you,
Write down all your secrets
And all your fears
On wisps of
Unlined paper,
Fold it three times
Away
From you
You may throw it,
As casually as you wish,
Into my flames

EL ARREPENTIMIENTO 0:
EL ARREPENTIMIENTO 0:

UNA POEMA QUE NUNCA SE MANDA
UNA POEMA QUE NUNCA SE MANDA

12/2023
12/2023

Como yo
No soy Neruda
Ni Beneditti
Ni Marti
No tengo rosa blanca
Cien Sonetas de amor
No te puedo escribir

No se explicarte
Que yo arrepenti

No me miras
No lo piensas

Creo que no me amas más
Mi recuerdo lo perdistes

Cuando llegó la cólera

Mi Cielito todavía
Estoy parada en la
Ciudad

De mi sueño
Rodeado de olas
Altas rompiendo
Nuestra paz

Mi cuerpo pequeña
Perdida entre las

Ruinas antiguas de allá
Yo sola estoy ahogada
Con la memoria
De cuando estaba

Segura sin frio

Dormida en tus brazos
Esa lejana mañana
De nuestra soledad

LOVE WITCH IN ACTION

7/2014

Dreams
Shuffling cards flutter
My arms as plumes of smoke
I see everything

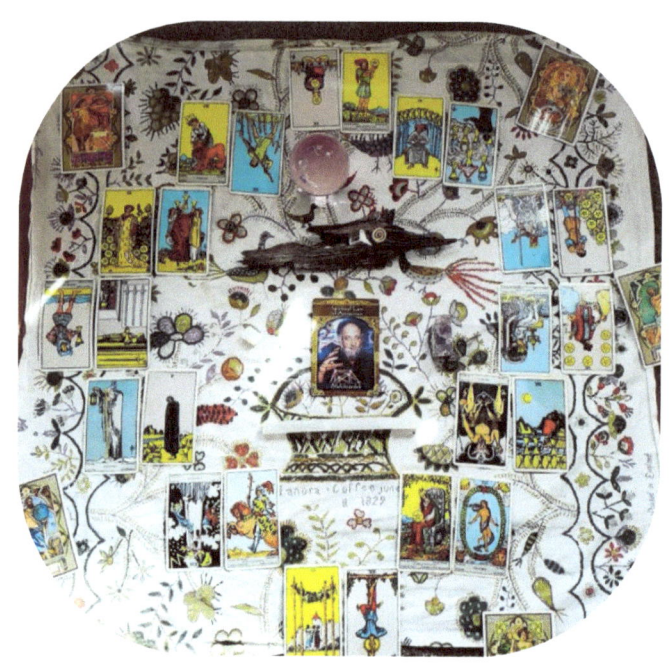

LOVE ON LOAN

01/2024

Broken Heart
exploits every pain
When life throws you lemons
Squeeze'em &
Sell'em &
Spend all the gains

Charge love
To the account &
When that bill comes back
Crumple & chuck it
And make that heart unmask

MORE THAN SORRY

12/2023

I shout across the canyon
I have been going on a spree
I write you a million poems
I throw a bottle in the sea

I smear my mortar down
One by one I lay the brick
I will build this bridge again
Even if it makes me sick

I swallow all my pride
Kick my ego to the curb
Every poem is an apology
& I mean every word

TWIN FLAME RUNNER

12/2023

If we ever found
Some time alone
I'd look you dead
In your eyes
Id say
I'm sorry
I'd say you hurt me
I'd say
I was angry

The Anger did not exterminate
What had taken deep root in
My heart
The Anger wasn't poison enough

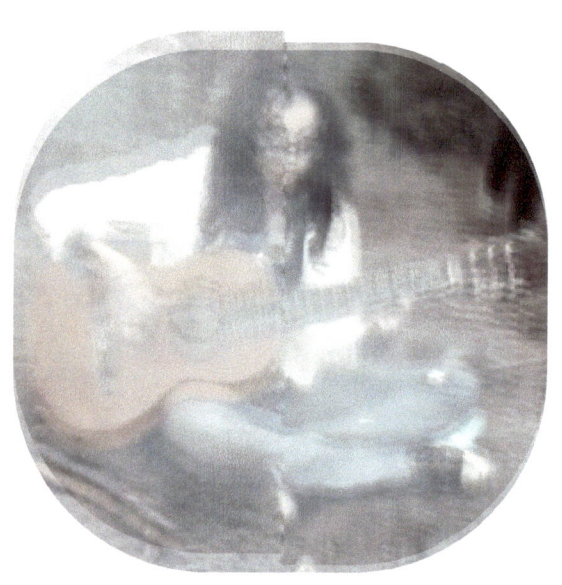

I sing you songs
In a language
You do not understand
I hide though
I cannot hide this
I cannot help myself

I'd say
This love for you
Will beam from me
Everytime you pass me by
You'll know
You'll say to yourself;
"There she goes,
A woman that will
Love me; until the day she dies:"

OBSERVACIÓN DE LA CÓLERA O:

OBSERVACIÓN DE LA CÓLERA O:

The Ambivalence of the Malcontented
The Ambivalence of the Malcontented

12/2024
12/2024

Breath bated,
Breath bated,
Broken and withheld
Broken and withheld

Mis terrores me han congelado
Mis terrores me han congelado
Ya no se ven estrellas en el cielo
Ya no se ven estrellas en el cielo
Las nubes lamentan
Las nubes lamentan
Lloran por mi
Lloran por mi

Anger is a mean
Anger is a mean
Red thing
Red thing
Edged on all sides
Edged on all sides
Whet ground on
Whet ground on
Passion's stone
Passion's stone

La tristeza es una sábana viscosa
La tristeza es una sábana viscosa
Que sueña con alquimizarse
Que sueña con alquimizarse
Hasta convertirse en seda
Hasta convertirse en seda

Armed
Armed
Sat exhausted
Sat exhausted
Flanked by shadows
Flanked by shadows
Moon cast
Moon cast

Te extraño, Mi Cielo.
Te extraño, Mi Cielo.

THE HIEROPHANT & THE THREE OF SWORDS

10/2023

I didn't realize
I'd left so much behind

Todo lo que he perdido

The tattered book that sang to me
A bracelet of raindrops
My wallet full of
Cash & Coins
I didn't know I'd need it
I wasn't warned
My *Abuela's* crucifix
My *Madrina's* rosary
The love we had
That was not yet wounded
When you loved more than
Just my cool shadow
Beneath your feet
In the age when
You loved me for my heat

-Y así cayó la estrella del cielo.

I followed
Running I dropped my
Watch
Time couldn't touch me
I danced
With no direction
And off came all my jewels
Fallen
Stomped into the sand
Only the smallest glimmer
In the fire light

When the river washed over me
I felt him in the water
I thought that I might drown

I didn't realize
I'd left so much behind
I traded voraciousness
For prudence
For control of appetite
It's not mindfulness
It's starvation
-¡Ay, Ay Cielo mío, debo rescatarte de la oscuridad!

TOWNSFOLK
TOWNSFOLK
04/24/2024
04/24/2024

Never
Never
Fall out of love
Fall out of love
I hope you stay that way
I hope you stay that way

I built a city in
I built a city in
My heart
My heart
For you
For you

There is a passage
There is a passage
In between us
In between us
Travel through
Travel through

I hand you the key to the city
I hand you the key to the city
You are
You are
Mayor & constituent
Mayor & constituent
Thanksgiving parade float,
Thanksgiving parade float,
Union leader,
Union leader,
Community gardener,
Community gardener,
Mail man
Mail man

There is a passage between
There is a passage between
You & me
You & me
I built you this city from the labor of dreams
I built you this city from the labor of dreams

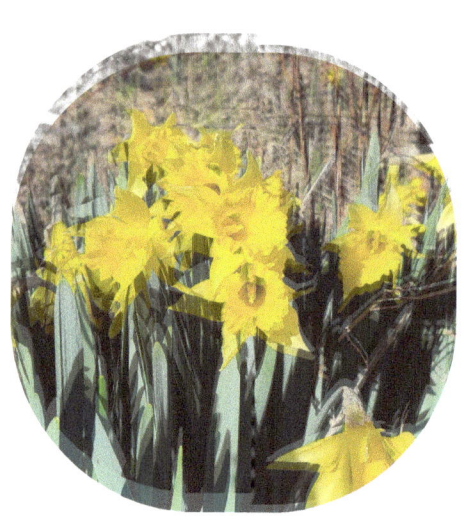

Sometimes
Sometimes
I take a hike there
I take a hike there
I sneak a peak
I sneak a peak
I look around
I look around
Leave gifts like a cat
Leave gifts like a cat
At your door
At your door
I see you dreaming
I see you dreaming
I give a little wave
I give a little wave
I post notes on the
I post notes on the
Bulletin board
Bulletin board
I see us in the windows
I see us in the windows
Of your house
Of your house

Worshiping together
Worshiping together
At the altar of community
At the altar of community

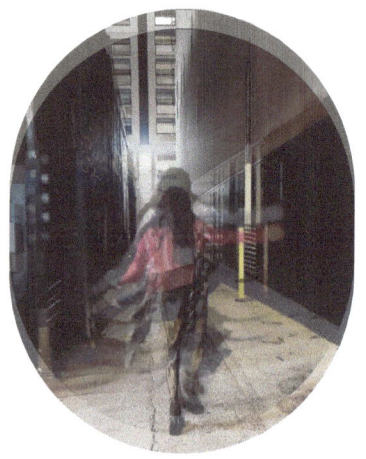

LOST IN TRANSLATION

12/2023
12/2023

Bea shouts,
Bea shouts,
"Spanish teacher!
"Spanish teacher!
How do you say heart?
How do you say heart?
I say,
I say,
-"Pedacitos en el agua."
-"Pedacitos en el agua."

She asks,
She asks,
"How do you say pear?"
"How do you say pear?"
I say,
I say,
-"Mi cuerpo bajo el árbol"
-"Mi cuerpo bajo el árbol"

Hugo turns,
Hugo turns,
"How do you say Volcano?"
"How do you say Volcano?"
I turn,
I turn,
-"El corazón es una isla en el mar."
-"El corazón es una isla en el mar."

Virginia taps me,
Virginia taps me,
"Spanish teacher,
"Spanish teacher,
Why do you walk with
Why do you walk with
Your hands inside your pockets
Your hands inside your pockets
And your eyes down on your feet?"
And your eyes down on your feet?"

I kneel to her, eye catching eye, I say
I kneel to her, eye catching eye, I say
-"Porque mis pies conservan
-"Porque mis pies conservan
Un gran anhelo,
Un gran anhelo,
Ellos bailan aunque no lo ves.
Ellos bailan aunque no lo ves.
En mis bolsillos
En mis bolsillos
Con cada mano aguanto
Con cada mano aguanto
A un sueño de amor que
A un sueño de amor que
No puede ser."
No puede ser."

III:

SOULMATE MEANS

FOREVER

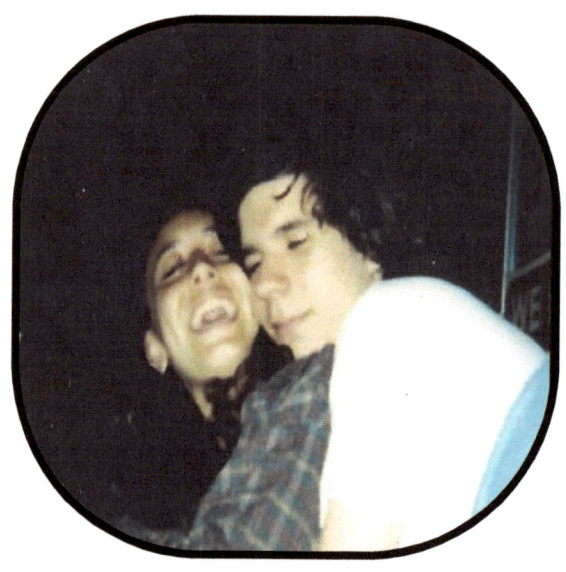

"When love beckons to you, follow him,
Though his ways are hard and steep.
And when his wings enfold you yield to
him...."
-Kahlil Gibran

I WROTE YOU A SONNET

05/18/2012

Were you to be Adonis
And I his Venus fair,
We would with Love abound
Pulling Cupid by his hairs
With neither pother from our mouths
Us with ne'er idle hands
We build our shelter here
Where mystery be the land
I would be your darling deer
"On mountain or in dale"
And I would live without fear
Nearer to you, hunter who dared.

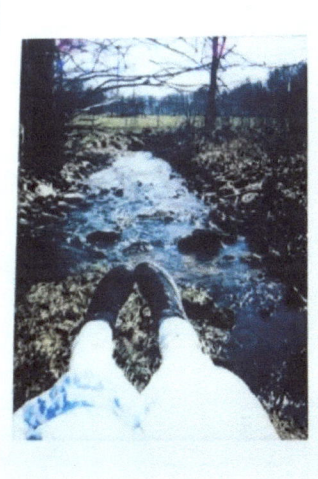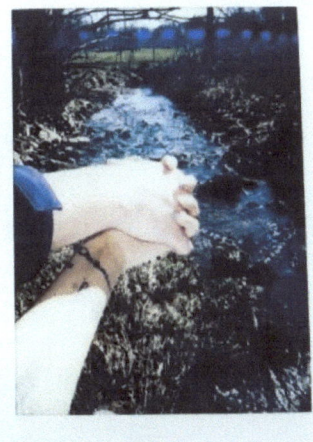

HEARTS OF THE TRUEST BELIEVERS

02/2024

I believe in our hands
Writers of poems and punch lines
They cradle fistfuls of intention
Curators of creative current
Moving us as we are allowed our tooling

AT LAST, OUR DAWN
AT LAST, OUR DAWN

03/2014
03/2014

You are my comrade
You are my comrade
We are ready for war
We are ready for war
My friend
My friend
Cosmic someone who
Cosmic someone who
Walks beside me through
Walks beside me through
The valley of selves
The valley of selves

We two sphinxes share
We two sphinxes share
Our riddles, our puzzles, our voice
Our riddles, our puzzles, our voice
We have learned
We have learned
Each others alchemy
Each others alchemy
Equivalent exchanges
Equivalent exchanges
travel between our hands
travel between our hands

What is taken
What is taken
Is given back
Is given back
What I give to you
What I give to you
Began as yours
Began as yours
Yours was mine
Yours was mine
Ours is acres, leagues
Ours is acres, leagues
Infinite and expansive
Infinite and expansive
All of it is for us
All of it is for us

Your fingers
Your fingers
enveloping philosophers
enveloping philosophers
Stones
Stones
This is the portrait
This is the portrait
That hangs above me
That hangs above me

My heart
My heart
Like a leaping fish
Like a leaping fish
Lunges through the air to
Lunges through the air to
Lay itself down, quietly
Lay itself down, quietly
Upon your mandible
Upon your mandible
Within the clenching jowls
Within the clenching jowls
Of your passion's dreams
Of your passion's dreams

I am an earthquake
I am an earthquake
You choose to caress
You choose to caress
The trembling tectonics
The trembling tectonics
That move me
That move me
I am not fixed, though
I am not fixed, though
I grow roots
I grow roots
Which you tug at
Which you tug at
Like kite strings
Like kite strings
As I flutter around the
As I flutter around the
Thunder clouds
Thunder clouds
Saving me from
Saving me from
Lightning
Lightning

You keep me safe
You keep me safe
You hide me within the
You hide me within the
Palpitations of your heart
Palpitations of your heart
Where I am allowed to
Where I am allowed to
Resonate as I burn
Resonate as I burn
As I burn
As I burn
I am
I am
Snaking through you
Snaking through you
I am a worm
I am a worm

A storm that in it's
A storm that in it's
Billowing
Billowing
Shakes your four walls
Shakes your four walls
And muddies your floor
And muddies your floor

I take you with me
I take you with me
I follow
I follow

My heart's a stowaway
My heart's a stowaway
I wear your love upon my skin
I wear your love upon my skin
I wear your kisses
I wear your kisses
Perfumed in them
Perfumed in them
I rub them into my pores
I rub them into my pores
Your glances stuff my bones
Your glances stuff my bones
Your scent has my face
Your scent has my face
Meandering through a land
Meandering through a land
Of pillows
Of pillows
Where you have been
Where you have been
Where we have slept
Where we have slept

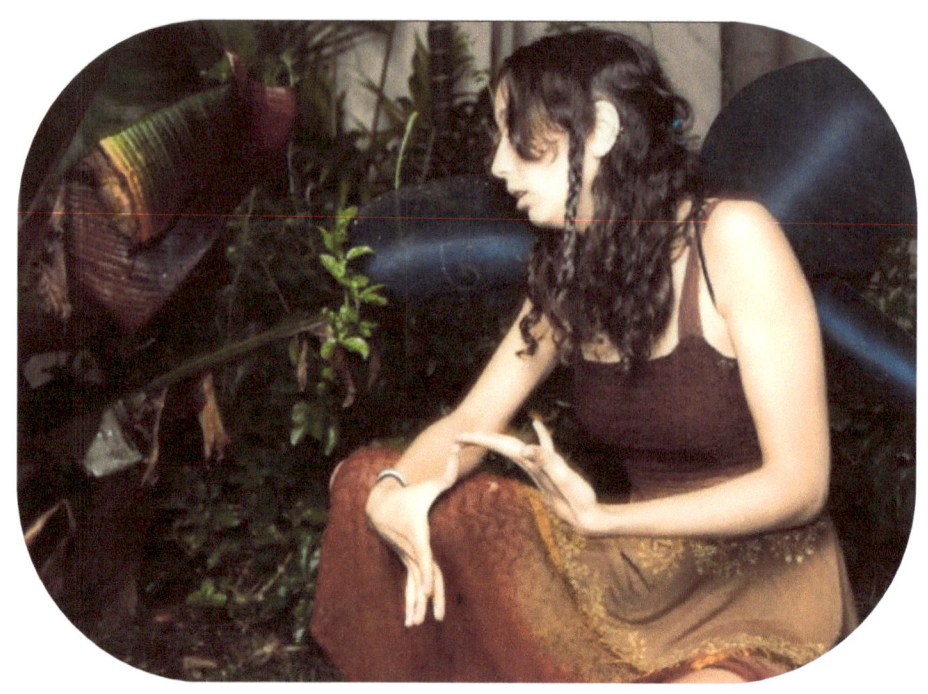

SAID THE WITCH TO THE WARRIOR

3/29/14

You want my pretty words
My darling
Pretty words are not enough for you
Fine praises, flattery, admiration,
They are but pastries comprised of products
Older than ourselves

Here, gentle whoever you are,
Take these, my small offerings
Sift through the minutiae of my love
I haven't any great strategy
Only this whetstone upon which I sharpen your sword
A knowledge of herbs with which to heal you
Tell me again just how beautiful I am
And I will walk alongside you
Until you find the forever you seek

A LETTER:
I SNEAK UNDER YOUR DOOR

12/2013

My darling one,
I eat off your plate.
My Love.
I sit by your door
I drink from your cup.
My Love.
I drink from your cup and
My Love,
I imagine you as you are
Sipping, slipping and spinning
You are dreaming
And I am watching
My Love.
I linger with your
Fork, with
Your spoon
I think of you and in My
Thoughts you are dreaming
You feel in your dreaming
I dream
Of your feelings
Every day my thinking
Covers you in kisses
Softly, my Love, softly
Do you even imagine what my, "I Love You" truly means?

It is an unfathomable sentiment
It is an unfathomable sentiment
It is so real it fills you
It is so real it fills you
You do not know why
You do not know why
It is so full you
It is so full you
Cannot bear it
Cannot bear it
Grasp it tightly
Grasp it tightly
I love you and I see you and
I love you and I see you and
I scare you
I scare you
Sometime it makes me laugh
Sometime it makes me laugh
When I say, "I love you my darling one,"
When I say, "I love you my darling one,"
I really mean to say
I really mean to say
I love to watch you live and
I love to watch you live and
Wonder
Wonder
To watch you love and
To watch you love and
Discover
Discover
You are fascinating
You are fascinating
And sincere
And sincere
I am glad to love you so utterly
I am glad to love you so utterly
I do not need your love's return to complete me
I do not need your love's return to complete me
Your being makes me happy
Your being makes me happy
Your introversion is flattering
Your introversion is flattering
Your questioning is becoming
Your questioning is becoming
Your smiling eyes shine handsomely
Your smiling eyes shine handsomely
I hope the finest women see you this way too:
I hope the finest women see you this way too:
I would hate to be the only woman to love you like I do:
I would hate to be the only woman to love you like I do:
Sincerely,
Sincerely,
Paola
Paola

P.S. If I could kiss you, my love,
P.S. If I could kiss you, my love,
My lips would write poems upon your lips:
My lips would write poems upon your lips:
I'd melt you.
I'd melt you.

OFFERING

OFFERING

04/29/07
04/29/07

This I write to my Muse,
This I write to my Muse,
Who tells stories with something
Who tells stories with something
Much more appealing
Much more appealing
Than words and gestures
Than words and gestures
Something much more
Something much more
Pleasing than sound
Pleasing than sound
The one who accompanies me
The one who accompanies me
Down this stretch of road-
Down this stretch of road-
(Past wretches and rich men
(Past wretches and rich men
Past an assortment of
Past an assortment of
Calamities and through
Calamities and through
The progression of days)
The progression of days)
-And sees the scorpion beneath the rock
-And sees the scorpion beneath the rock
Which conceals it
Which conceals it
The Muse who indulges
The Muse who indulges
In escape, whose legs are blue flames
In escape, whose legs are blue flames
Whose body illuminates and
Whose body illuminates and
Emanates the heat that
Emanates the heat that
Is not quite so fearsome
Is not quite so fearsome
Only comforting in the sense that
Only comforting in the sense that
It warms the frozen marrow of my bones
It warms the frozen marrow of my bones
And boils my blood with an intensity
And boils my blood with an intensity
One could compare to Icarus and the sun
One could compare to Icarus and the sun
A courier of inspiration
A courier of inspiration
A gardener who scatters the seeds
A gardener who scatters the seeds
Of peace profusely
Of peace profusely
In hopes that both something may sprout
In hopes that both something may sprout
There and that peace will be had
There and that peace will be had
I attempt to collect words
I attempt to collect words
As satiating as ripe fruits
As satiating as ripe fruits
That bend the branches of a tree
That bend the branches of a tree
Closer to the grass
Closer to the grass
Filled with a juice that may
Filled with a juice that may
Quench the parched lips of
Quench the parched lips of
Their receiver
Their receiver
Whose sweet meat
Whose sweet meat
May calm all hunger
May calm all hunger
And cause a great affinity
And cause a great affinity
For the collector,
For the collector,
The inspired
The inspired

MY SOULMATE IS HAUNTING HIMSELF OR: INDECISION MAKES INCISIONS IN HIS HEART

05/2023

I would feel as if
You've given up on me
But I feel that
I wasn't worth the try

I believe you love me
I always showed you how
You might have been busy
It might not have been
The right time

I believe you love me
I've been waiting
To see it show
You tell me all the time
But it feels like I don't know

Sometimes I can really tell
That your love for me is true
But most times I'm so lonely
Even when I'm together with you

I feel like I've been waiting
A decade or maybe more
For you to love me in the way
I need, want and deserve

LESSONS ON OBSERVATION

06/2006

I wonder where the wandering vehicles go
And from whence they came
To pass urgently down my street

He sits and watches them with me

The stump of the old umbrella tree
Grows damp and destroyed
But from it grows
Green ferns that wave
Brightly against the somber
Gray
Of the sky and the lake
The hawk soars on the
Cool wind, behind him
Clouds blowing east towards
The Gulf of Mexico
The small white ibis glides parallel to
The house across the way
The breeze makes me shiver
The sound of cars, birds and children
Flits through me, as the dead brown
Leaves tremble upon the branch above

He sees this too, his eyes lurking here with me

My cigarette tastes bland and uninviting
I think I will write poetry
Brew some tea and smoke a joint
The sun
In vain
Tries desperately to break through
The sea of clouds like the bones

Of the rotting water moccasin beside us
Washed up by the waters of
Galloway Lake
Pushing up out of it's skin
For a moment the sun shines brilliantly upon the lake
And dabbles it with jewels
Brightens the grass
The neighbor whistles at the dogs
Now the sun has just shone bright upon my head

He notices the sun upon me
He smiles

Everything's obscenely serene
I hear the old Cuban jazz emanating
From the house behind me
I notice the rust stains on the fence
The solitary rotten block of Styrofoam
A forgotten cup, a lost bracelet

He's noticed all this already

Where are the cars going?
Where are the cars going?
Where are the cars going?
Where are the cars going?
Where are the cars going?
Where are the cars going?
Where are the cars going?
Where are the cars going?

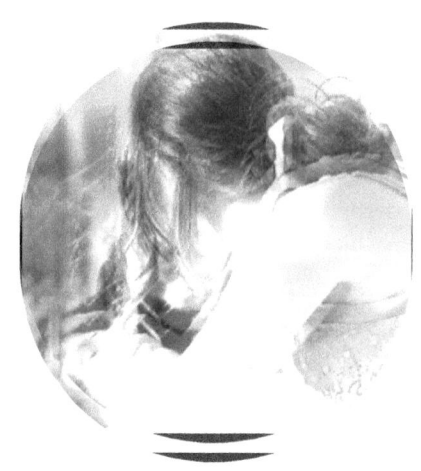

MARCOS
MARCOS

5/25/2006
5/25/2006

W/ eyes like river-washed pebbles
W/ eyes like river-washed pebbles

& hands like sun heated velvet,
& hands like sun heated velvet,

You have found the twisting, spinning path
You have found the twisting, spinning path

Too treacherous for anyone to have walked
Too treacherous for anyone to have walked

You,
You,

& your sweet words
& your sweet words

Creeping out of you like dragons breath
Creeping out of you like dragons breath

Casting friendly shadows that
Casting friendly shadows that

Envelope this cliché in contentment
Envelope this cliché in contentment

I find myself,
I find myself,

Sprawled languidly across your mind
Sprawled languidly across your mind

Counting rose petals like garden stones
Counting rose petals like garden stones

To tiptoe across in hopes,
To tiptoe across in hopes,

Of catching a glimpse of you
Of catching a glimpse of you

Soundly asleep and pleasantly nude
Soundly asleep and pleasantly nude

On the other side of this creek.
On the other side of this creek.

IV.

MY FATHER'S DAUGHTER,
MYSELF
IN WATERCOLOR &
THE FURIOUS SHADOW

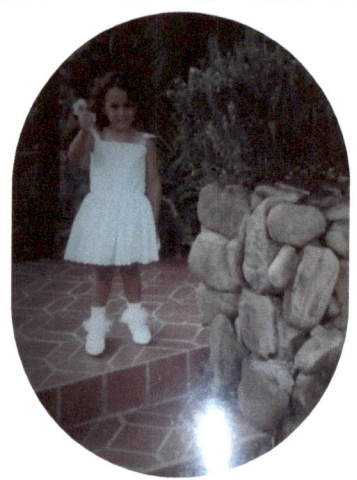

-ON MOST DAYS I'M A 5 1/2 FT FLESHY MESS OF
CONFUSION, CONTRADICTIONS, CONFLICTS AND CONSEQUENCE.
- I'M 108 LBS OF THE SAME RAW INGREDIENT FORMULA
AS WHOLE GALAXIES AND SOLAR NEBULAE.
-I VOICE MY OPINIONS SO THEY BOOM ACROSS THE GAPS
THAT ARE CREATED BY PEOPLE BETWEEN THEMSELVES AND OTHERS,
AS IT IS SIMULTANEOUSLY MUTED, MUDDLED AND MALIGNED.
- SO SOMETIMES I FEEL LIKE I'M WALKING ON
MY HANDS TO GO FASTER THOUGH I STILL
WEAR THESE INANE SKATES ON MY FEET.
-THESE ARE MY NAMES THOUGH
I AM NAMELESS, THOUGH I
AM FACELESS,
LOOK THROUGH MY FACE MAKE
ROOM IN YOUR FACE FOR MINE,
THERE IS ROOM IN MINE FOR YOURS...

CHANGE FOR A FIVE

12/31/2023

I'm floating through pools of "timelessness".

The winter, a professor,
Assigns me
A lesson on
introspection.
I procrastinate
I'm past the due date

New year approaches
Minutes away

The night, a courtesan
Sensual someone seduces
Self to sleep

New year tomorrow
I realize
I am not ashamed
To be starting again
I know what I've done
& I know very well
What I need to do

PLIGHT OF THE SENTIENT ANACHRONISM
~~PLIGHT OF THE SENTIENT ANACHRONISM OR:~~

~~I AM A GIRL OF CIRCUMSTANCE PART II~~

12-21-2013
12-21-2013

Dame un cortado
Pero no,
Por favor mi vida,
No me cortes
Ni un deseo
Ni un sueño tengo
De bailar
Con tus cuchillos
Ni pedir prestado
Tus alas de luz
Blanco
Tu orgullo pesado
Tu vuelo de mariposa
Borracha y viciosa
I want a cortadito
I say
Half sugar
Half milk,
Honey make it
Without the
Foam
Thank you
'De donde eres?'
I'm from here
Could you sprinkle in

Some cinnamon please?
Some cinnamon please?
¿Tienen Canela?
¿Tienen Canela?
Dame un cortadito
Dame un cortadito
Porfavor
Porfavor
con un chin de sal
con un chin de sal
un tilin de sal
un tilin de sal
I'm from here
I'm from here
Claro que
Claro que
Sí,
Sí,
Bien oscuro
Bien oscuro
Gracias
Gracias
No lo quiero miti miti
No lo quiero miti miti
I would like it rather dark
I would like it rather dark
I want more coffee than milk
I want more coffee than milk
I would like it very dark
I would like it very dark
Actually
Actually
No
No
Scratch the milk
Scratch the milk
I'd like it with heavy cream
I'd like it with heavy cream
More coffee than cream
More coffee than cream
More fat than water
More fat than water
What can I say I'm a hedonist
What can I say I'm a hedonist
I walk the streets of
I walk the streets of
Miami proper
Miami proper
As if they were mine
As if they were mine
Me crie aka
Me crie aka
Cubana
Cubana
Dominicana
Dominicana
De Kendall
De Kendall
Por Dadeland
Por Dadeland
These streets I
These streets I
Stomp upon and litter
Stomp upon and litter
Upon
Upon
Frivolously
Frivolously
With
With
The crumbled remains of
The crumbled remains of
My adolescent frivolity
My adolescent frivolity

As if I could own these streets
Weren't for their existence
Beneath my feet
They
The streets
They probably
Wouldn't exist at all
-Said the anachronistic effeminately displaced
Modern day Narcissus
During a conversation with
Herself

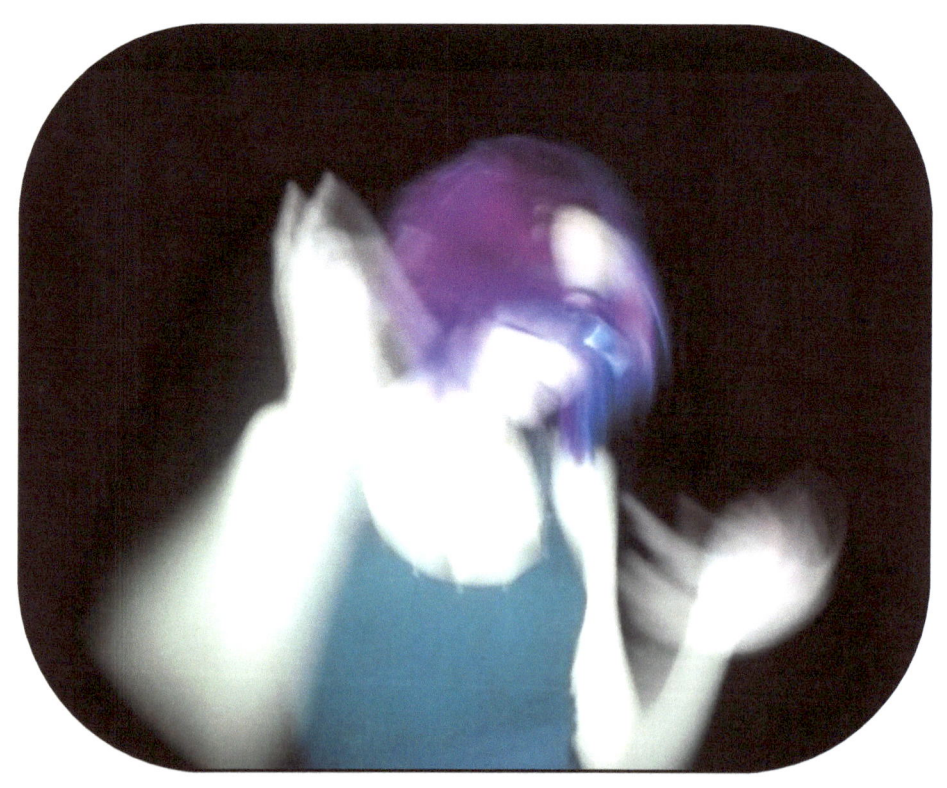

TRAVELING STATES FAIR

02/17/2009

Th' ice cream truck
Ain't playin' non' o' that
Dixie land jazz
Wish it smelt mo'
Like prize winning pie
As 'pposed to th'
Reek of th' pettin' zoo
I'm'a gerbil
With a new
Blue ribbon
I won it all by m'self
Don't fit in any
Hamster wheel
Oh no! Oh no!
And I'm jus' fine with that
Th' ice cream truck
Sound like'a carousel
The wind's makin' love
To the sun
In My-yami
At four o'clock pm
When it's silent
In February
Time for Ferris wheels!
Not for sleep.
Time for singin'!
Don't you dare dance boy
I've seen'em slice a man
At the ankles for dancing
'Round this time o' year
Left'em for dead
Or at least
Suffocatin' on hay
And doused in blue paint

THIS IS THE WAY MY GARDEN GROWS
~~THIS IS THE WAY MY GARDEN GROWS OR:~~
THE BOTANY OF BROKEN THINGS
~~THE BOTANY OF BROKEN THINGS~~

02/26/14
02/26/14

I do not wear
I do not wear
Gloves when I garden
Gloves when I garden
My hands are covered in desire
My hands are covered in desire
When I rise in the morning
When I rise in the morning
I cease to be the
I cease to be the
Ghost of myself that
Ghost of myself that
Has been haunting
Has been haunting
My friends
My friends
Incessantly
Incessantly
I don't wear clothing
I don't wear clothing
When I garden
When I garden
My body is made of mud
My body is made of mud
Any how
Any how
I want to feel closer to God
I want to feel closer to God
So the earthworm lends me
So the earthworm lends me
His form and in his dress
His form and in his dress
I need not wear a mask
I need not wear a mask
Nor rouge nor liner
Nor rouge nor liner
Oh no
Oh no
I need not wear a mask
I need not wear a mask
The sheerness of my fear is enough
The sheerness of my fear is enough
It is the sun
It is the sun
The sun on my back
The sun on my back
That encourages me to pull
That encourages me to pull
The weeds from their roots
The weeds from their roots

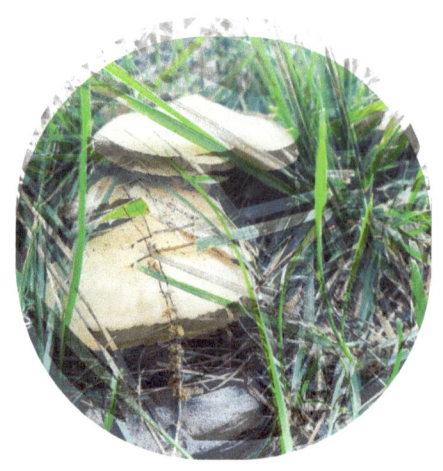

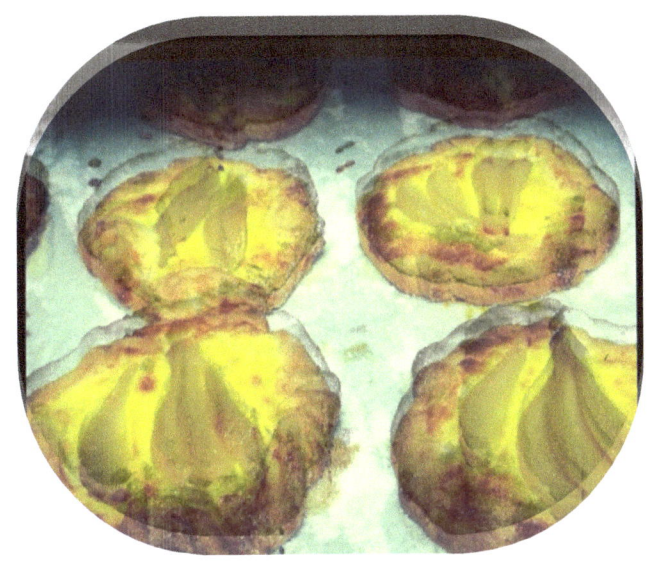

BAKE SALE
BAKE SALE
08/2016
08/2016

I make pastries
I make pastries
To buy time for poems
To buy time for poems
Poems are sweet little mouthfuls
Poems are sweet little mouthfuls
I write them down
I write them down
I don't care why
I don't care why
They are for after dinner
They are for after dinner
And for before bed
And for before bed
Poems are sweets the soul craves
Poems are sweets the soul craves
Infinite
Infinite
A poem performed through forever
A poem performed through forever
A pastry perpetual
A pastry perpetual

PLUMP
PLUMP
AND CRISP
AND CRISP

SHADOW BOXING THE ENEMY

09/2013

Every night
During the shifting of the sky
I leave out a
Glass of wine
For her
I fear
She has taken refuge
In the oven
She flattens my pastries into crumbs
She stirs my casseroles so that they
Never crisp
I leave out a glass of wine for her
As an apology
For all the things I will
Eventually
Do,
Have done,
Thought of.

That damned ghost
Drinks my wine
And let's grease drip, drip
sizzle
In order to set her hair
On fire
Because she's
Afraid
And she's avoiding the sun

She can not understand a literal anything
For she is fashioned from simile and
Lives as many lives as she can dream
While rotting and dying
Simultaneously

This is a metaphor for the
Birds
The ones outside my window
While I sleep, she invites them to eat
Syntax and diction in the
Form of sweet crumbs and stories
She
Phantasm fiend
Advises the worms
To ignore the soft subtlety of my symmetry
And they stand alone
And leave their chalky carcasses
In the sun, on the sidewalk
I believe they are in cahoots
With her,
With the raccoons
I believe they carry
Hefty bags of my organs
Back to head quarters
Where they stash the harvest
Moon and dance
Am I her golem?
Am I her silhouette?
When I awake,
There are coffee stains upon the floor
I feel a hair on my tongue that I can not pick off
There are claw marks on the door
There is a bandits mask hanging from its ribbon on the knob

TO THE VICTOR GO THE SPOILS

TO THE VICTOR GO THE SPOILS

10/22/13
10/22/13

Never became the Victor he had hoped to be
Never became the Victor he had hoped to be
Triumph came only through words valedictory
Triumph came only through words valedictory
This was our non-victorious victor's victory
This was our non-victorious victor's victory

Never won his right to glory
Never won his right to glory
Only scrap heaps in the fray
Only scrap heaps in the fray
He fiercely stuffed within
He fiercely stuffed within
His bones of justifiable decay
His bones of justifiable decay

Never enough sadness in his jeers
Never enough sadness in his jeers
As there actually should have been
As there actually should have been
Never enough joy to sate his tears
Never enough joy to sate his tears
Or enough solemn silence in his din
Or enough solemn silence in his din

Never enough God or spirits holy
Never enough God or spirits holy
In his mouth, his eyes, his ears
In his mouth, his eyes, his ears
Never enough fragrance flowing
Never enough fragrance flowing
From the fathoms of his fears
From the fathoms of his fears

Never enough wind within his wink
Never enough wind within his wink
Never enough things for him to think
Never enough things for him to think
Never enough depths for him to sink
Never enough depths for him to sink

Yet
Yet

He did have many a fine "however"
He did have many a fine "however"
He had a myriad "never-enoughs"
He had a myriad "never-enoughs"
He burned them with the kindling
He burned them with the kindling
Of his passion's driest brush
Of his passion's driest brush

As a little girl he seemed to me
As a little girl he seemed to me
So small in all his sitting
So small in all his sitting
Unraveling, itching and picking
Unraveling, itching and picking
The strings of my frail binding
The strings of my frail binding
Casually confident in his coaxing
Casually confident in his coaxing
Perpetually loafing and watching
Perpetually loafing and watching
His Zenith, his Acer, his Sony
His Zenith, his Acer, his Sony

I learned so much from the sight
I learned so much from the sight
Of his learning nothing whatsoever
Of his learning nothing whatsoever
His skin shed him every night
His skin shed him every night
The devil delt him clever swelters
The devil delt him clever swelters

For twelve long years I suckled
For twelve long years I suckled
Naivety from his negligent defeats
Naivety from his negligent defeats
I dined on his dissonant chuckles
I dined on his dissonant chuckles
I ate the crumbs falling to his feet
I ate the crumbs falling to his feet

Though he was never
Though he was never
Never there and
Never there and
Though feigning, feigning
Though feigning, feigning
That he cared
That he cared
This victor appeared to me
This victor appeared to me
He appeared everywhere
He appeared everywhere
Everywhere, everywhere
Everywhere, everywhere

Even between the letters
Even between the letters
On the pages of my books
On the pages of my books
Where I hid from him for days
Where I hid from him for days
Where he never thought to look
Where he never thought to look

He was hiding always there
He was hiding always there
In the bellowing of the breeze
In the bellowing of the breeze
In the space below the stairs
In the space below the stairs
In foggy palaces of forgotten keys
In foggy palaces of forgotten keys

Pretentious pop
Seeing him never stops
I see him at the quick shop
In the spinning of my top
In the habits that I drop

I see him

At the bottoms of flat beers
In the reflections of the years
In the totters my mind teeters
In songs of eggs and beaters

In the macabre musings of my mayhem
In strange responses to shalom aleichem
In the pleat of every skirt I unhem
In the petaled pedestal of every stem

I see him, still, I see him

I swear, I swear, I swear
He has not the faintest whim
That I see him even where

He knows all of my secrets
I can sing every one of his
He doesn't even know this
Wouldn't get it if he did
I
Recite all his Discrepancies
I
Place upon them melodies
I find within them poetry
Truth, congruence, symmetry

These are the many poems
He never thought to write
I have written them for him
So I recite them, I recite
They transformed to seeds
One day they rid Self of plight

Not one will I dare
Scatter, sow or share
To whom they belong
Will convert seed to song

The greatest truth I've ever known
Is that every seed has potential to grow

For
Victor Esteban Tavarez
1971-2022

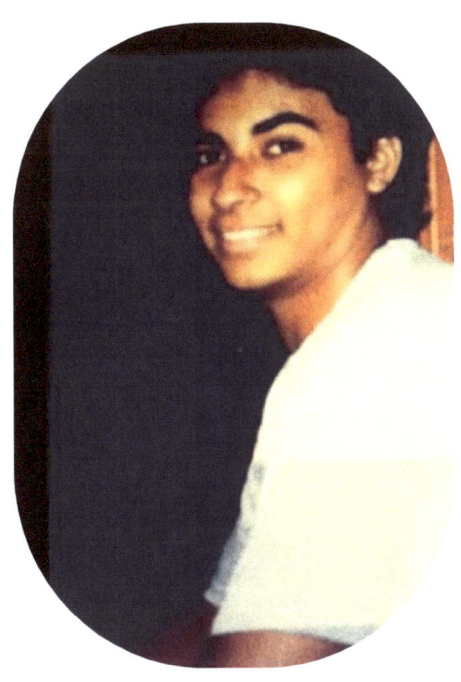

A PRESENTATION ON OBSERVATIVE SEXUAL ~~PSEUDO~~ PSYCHOLOGY

3/20/2012

I have a chronic case of
sleeping with men I,
Quite frankly,
Do not understand in the least

I have a recurring dream
Of falling asleep with someone
And then suddenly
Waking up alone

When I was a little girl
My father told me the meaning of
Life was to eat food and have sex
That everything else in life is a way
To pass the time between eating
And fucking

Eating and fucking,
I thought,
"Huh, well..."

My *Madrina* taught me that
If you hold the hair dryer up to the
Foggy bathroom mirror
You could make a window to
See yourself in

My first love and I
Blew neighboring windows
Onto the bathroom mirror
Of our first and only home
Just to stare at each other while we
Brushed our teeth

I find that having sex with men who I don't
Understand is almost like an anthropological
Study, a man reveals himself when he grunts,
Does he hold my face, is there a point where kissing
Stops, will we cuddle afterward?

How long they feel Comfortable being completely naked after an
orgasm
Seems to define their level of emotional attraction
If they sleep over but quickly get dressed when they wake and leave
while
You're still rubbing the gunk out of your eyes
I must say you shouldn't expect any calls

I was 17 when I first fell in love
Prudish, an amateur masturbator
Not a big fan of fellatio or
Hand jobs

I dreamt of us living in a
Punk rock mansion
A mattress with no bed sheets
One pillow, one towel
A dog and five cats
Tattoos and whippets
Joints and old records
Long nights on the beach looking for aliens

I think that in not understanding the men I sleep with
I am allowing for truly subjective scientific observation
The details of a man are what make him
Nail biter, long toe nails, keeps his socks on during sex,
Silent when he cums, snores,
Sleeps with music on, sleeps with tv on, sleeps in silence,
Says, "gorgeous, little lady, cute, adorable, fine,"
Drives a car, rides a bike, doesn't eat vegetables,
Alcoholic, artist, lives with parents,
Went to college, GED, looks me in the eyes,
Runs his fingers through my hair

My first love said
I had the nose of a mako shark
Four years after we first met
He started telling me to brush my teeth more often
We didn't make fog windows to see each other in
Anymore
I caught him with a fat chested girl
She had stretch marks around her nipples
I was pretty upset

My father always said
"Honey, I hate to be alone, you
Know your dad can't be alone."
We used to watch Teenage Mutant Ninja Turtles
Right after Bill Nay the Science Guy
On Saturdays
While my mother sprinkled that Arm & Hammer
Vacuum powder stuff onto the floor
Dad always made the best bowl of fruit loops in the world
Last time we spoke he said,
"It's not falling asleep alone,
It's waking up alone that kills us."

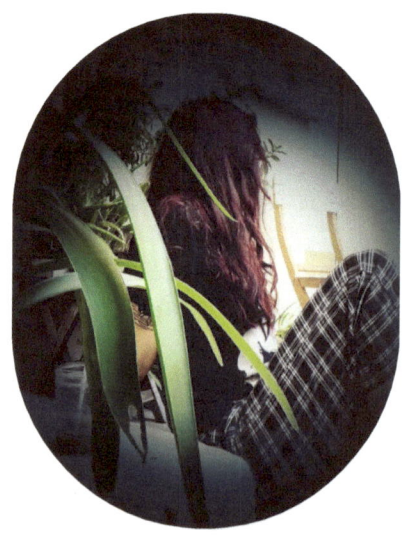

HOW IT USED TO BE: AIRPORT POEMS

6/21/2023

It used to be all palm trees and bubble gum bubbles
It used to be all roller skates and summer all year round
It used to be sand in the car and
hot seats that stick to your thighs
It used to be just so god damn hot all the time

And one day
I felt a cool breeze blow by
It was so refreshing, soft and wafting
It grabbed me like a mother cat
By the scruff
It carried me away

It use to be all poetry and cocaine
Blue eyeshadow and short girls
It used to be red lipstick and
UFO sightings on the beach, at dawn
It used to be that the things that used to be
Would be the things that would be
Forever and ever and ever.

It used to be that poems woke up me in the middle of my sleep
It used to be that my Muse had a very anxious attachment style
It used to be that my Muse was toxic and mean

i can't quite remember when the things that used to be
I can't quite remember when the things that used to be
Ceased to be
Ceased to be
Changed
Changed
Shifted
Shifted
I can't quite put my finger on it
I can't quite put my finger on it
When was the precise day my Muse woke
When was the precise day my Muse woke
Me up in my sleep and instead of
Me up in my sleep and instead of
Jumping to my pen
Jumping to my pen
I shoo-ed her away, again and again
I shoo-ed her away, again and again

It used to be people watching on Collins Ave
It used to be people watching on Collins Ave
It used to be riding the train just to watch
It used to be riding the train just to watch
Everyone living their lives
Everyone living their lives
The city passing me by
The city passing me by
It used to be writing all of that down
It used to be writing all of that down
All the time
All the time
No matter what
No matter what

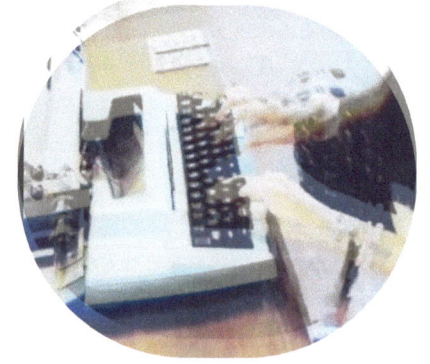

FEAR IS NOT ENOUGH, IT MUST BE WRITTEN AS WELL

August 4, 2023

When I write
Sat, scrunched, furrowed

Every wind which
Throughout history has blown
Whistled, whirled
& rustled

Every ray & beam &
Washing of the light
Casting & erasing
Long, long shadows

Every wave
Each ebb & flow
The crashing, the stillness
Every reflection of the moon
Upon every surface that
Can Catch

Every massive storm
That has
Ever
Devastated man

Combine
Within
Suddenly
My hands
Are left with no
Choice

As I am
Sat, scrunched, furrowed
My hands
Move
Until the writing is all done

I AM A GIRL OF CIRCUMSTANCE

06/2010

Given the circumstance
Of my existence,
I count my blessing
On the tip of each toe
Concealed in sock and shoe,
Along with the lunch money
No one will ever find.
Given the circumstances
In which I live;
Sunrise
Sunset
Sunrise
Sunset
Waxing and
Waning moons-
I resent all walls
For the sheer audacity of their
Remaining so solemnly solid.
I resent all ceilings
For their way
Of keeping the rain from my hair,
And the sun
From my skin:
Ceiling fans, for
Their melancholy attempt
To recreate the sensation of a cool breeze

A NEW YEAR POEM
MEMORANDUMS: OR DRINKING ALONE ON NEW YEARS

1/1/14

1. Never drink alone
2. Never forget the thing that heals you. It is for you to wield, it is a magic all your own. It is a code written within your blood. It cannot use you. You can only master it or watch it sleep.
3. You easily forget yourself. Stop that.
4. Poetry becomes you. Write at all costs.
5. There isn't much more for you to learn that must be done through gross self-flagellation.
6. Sex is good for you, but great conversation beats an orgasm.
7. When you wear a lovers face like a mask, do not forget, you had to remove your face before you put theirs on. If you've lost it, It is often in the place you last left it.
8. Respect the metaphors. They are not a crutch.
9. Never question your poems. Sometimes, they are not for you to understand.
10. Fear is not an excuse.
11. If you still regret it, then you have learned absolutely nothing from it.
12. Resistance is the enemy.
13. When you criticize yourself you stifle your sincerest truths.
14. You aren't made of water color.

14:

15: You aren't etched on the sides of the mountains either.

16: Taste is a language

17: A pastry is a poem you can eat.

18: Allow yourself

19: Trust deeply in your truths. Remember each one, learn them like a language. You will collect them as you go. They will always save you.

20: Decisions are cobble stones. We lay them down, we walk upon them. They echo our footsteps and wear out our shoes.

21: You are a product of the things you love multiplied by your constant and complete misunderstanding of them.

22: Everything I see is mine and also not mine. I own nothing and nothing owns me. Nothing will ever be my own. I do not belong to things. Things do not belong to me.

23: The songs of air conditioners amount to nothing compared to the symphony of winds.

24: Exhale the ship wrecks. When you imbibe in them they tend to upset your stomach and cause a mild hysteric lunacy. Makes for great poems but harmful to your health.

25: You are just as afraid of everything as everything is afraid of you.

26: Don't think so much, it's not good for you.

27: Believe in your poems, they trusted in you to deliver them. That is one of life's greatest honors.

2004

2004

TRUTH IS A LIE I WISH TO KNOW
TRUTH IS A LIE I WISH TO KNOW
KISS ME ONCE BEFORE I GO
KISS ME ONCE BEFORE I GO
THE STREETS ARE FILLED WITH SHALLOW POOLS
THE STREETS ARE FILLED WITH SHALLOW POOLS
THE AIR IS FILLED WITH LAUGHING FOOLS
THE AIR IS FILLED WITH LAUGHING FOOLS
CONCRETE NAMES ETCHED ON MY HEART
CONCRETE NAMES ETCHED ON MY HEART
WAS IT TRUE WE WOULD NEVER PART?
WAS IT TRUE WE WOULD NEVER PART?
SONGS OF YOU LOUD ON MY MIND
SONGS OF YOU LOUD ON MY MIND
THE WARMTH LOST I CANNOT FIND
THE WARMTH LOST I CANNOT FIND
BEAUTY TALKS LIKE A LANGUID DREAM
BEAUTY TALKS LIKE A LANGUID DREAM
AND WE DANCE ALONG A FLOWING STREAM
AND WE DANCE ALONG A FLOWING STREAM
WHY WOULD YOU RATHER CRY?
WHY WOULD YOU RATHER CRY?
LET US FLY LET US FLY
LET US FLY LET US FLY
WE DANCE LIKE NYMPHS WITH TINTED EYES
WE DANCE LIKE NYMPHS WITH TINTED EYES
YOUR IRIS LIKE SOMBER LULLABIES
YOUR IRIS LIKE SOMBER LULLABIES
TRUTH IS A LIE I WISH TO KNOW
TRUTH IS A LIE I WISH TO KNOW
KISS ME ONCE BEFORE I GO
KISS ME ONCE BEFORE I GO
MY VEINS ARE SHALLOW DANCE WITH WINE
MY VEINS ARE SHALLOW DANCE WITH WINE
THE MUSIC IS A GODDESS DIVINE
THE MUSIC IS A GODDESS DIVINE
THE MOON WHISPERS OF MY BIRTH
THE MOON WHISPERS OF MY BIRTH
HOW I SPRUNG UP FROM THE EARTH
HOW I SPRUNG UP FROM THE EARTH
KITTY, KITTY TELL ME YOUR TALE
KITTY, KITTY TELL ME YOUR TALE
YOUR LOVE LINE SHORT AND PALE
YOUR LOVE LINE SHORT AND PALE
KISS ME HERE KISS ME THERE
KISS ME HERE KISS ME THERE
KITTY FUNNY THINGS ARE EVERYWHERE
KITTY FUNNY THINGS ARE EVERYWHERE
TRUTH IS A LIE I WISH TO KNOW
TRUTH IS A LIE I WISH TO KNOW
KISS ME ONCE BEFORE I GO
KISS ME ONCE BEFORE I GO

photos by Volet Cabrera
photos by Volet Cabrera

THIS BOOK IS DEDICATED
TO EVERYONE I HAVE EVER LOVED,
TO MY LIFE PARTNER & OLDEST FRIEND,
MARCOS
TO THE LOVERS
DAY DREAMERS
& HOPELESS ROMANTICS
THE BROKEN HEARTED
THE BELIEVERS
THE ONES WITH NEVER ENDING FAITH
IN LOVE
&
TO THE ONE WHO STOLE MY HEART
& SET ME FREE SO THAT
THIS COLLECTION
COULD BE BORN UNTO THE SHELF
MAY YOU NEVER
EVER
FALL OUT OF LOVE

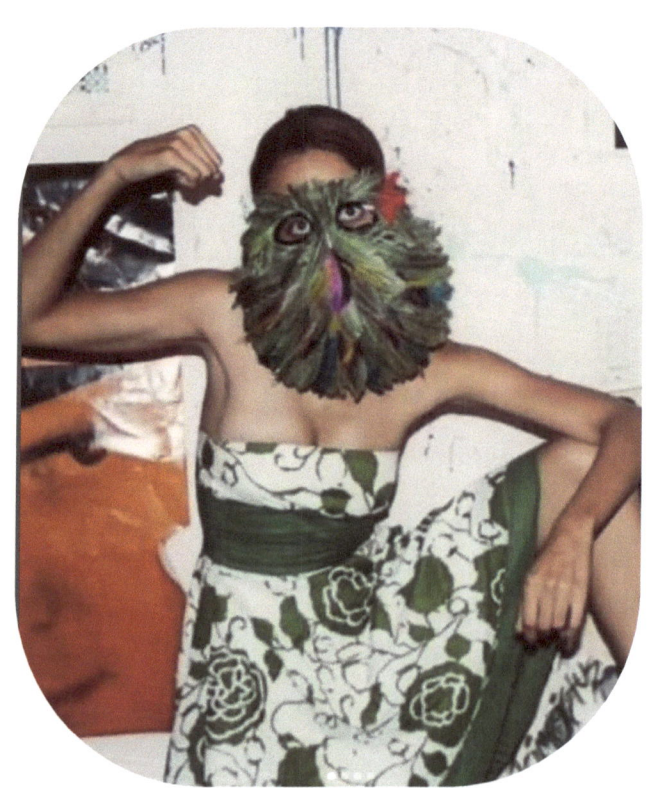